A Workshop with *Velda Newman*

ADDING DIMENSION
TO YOUR QUILTS

C&T PUBLISHING

© 2002 by Velda Newman
Editor: Cyndy Lyle Rymer
Technical Editor: Peggy Kass
Copyeditor/Proofreader: Peggy Kass, Susan Nelson
Cover Designer: Aliza Shalit
Design Director/Book Designer: Aliza Shalit
Illustrator: Richard Sheppard
Production Assistant: Kirstie L. McCormick
Photography: Steven Buckley, Photographic Reflections,
unless otherwise noted
Published by C&T Publishing, Inc., P.O. Box 1456,
Lafayette, California 94549

Front cover: Detail of *Hollyhocks*
(full quilt on pages 66–67), 2001

Back cover: *Tulip Study* by Velda Newman

Library of Congress Cataloging-in-Publication Data
Newman, Velda
  A workshop with Velda Newman : adding dimension to
your quilts / Velda E. Newman.
      p. cm.
Includes bibliographical references and index.
  ISBN 1-57120-185-8 (paper trade)
  1. Quilts—Design. 2. Color in textile crafts. 3. Textile
painting.
I. Title.
  TT835 .N48523 2002
  746.46—dc21
                              2002001398

Printed in Singapore
10 9 8 7 6 5 4 3 2 1

California Gold, 24" x 36", 1997
Techniques used: Shape and
Texture Stitching, Paint,
Watercolor Pencil

For Christina, Amber, and Paula
For my granddaughters Payden, Reid, and Riley
For my sister, Heidi
For my friend since kindergarten, Betty
And with special thanks to my daughter Heather

Contents

Asheville Quilt Guild
P.O. Box 412 Asheville, NC 28802

Preface

There are as many ways to approach design as there are designers. Although I offer projects, ultimately this book is to help you find your own path. In the first section I introduce you to the basic design elements of color, shape, and texture. By understanding these three main ingredients, your design process should become more direct and ultimately more successful. I encourage you to look for inspiration in all places. It often seems that getting started is the most difficult part of the design process, but it doesn't have to be. By opening yourself up to the color, shape, and texture of the world around you, you will find a wealth of amazing subjects. Pay attention to the details and you will have to do little more than translate these elements into the pieces you create with the help of this book. The world will have done most of the work for you.

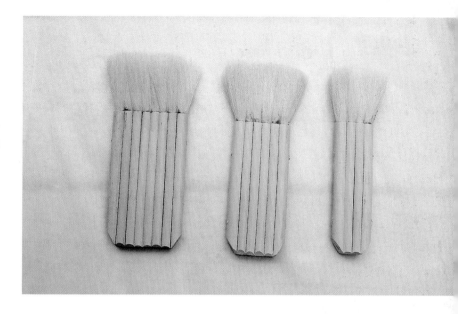

Six techniques are included in the second section of the book. These are the staple techniques I have come to rely on for creating color, shape, and texture. Begin by reading through the process for each technique. Some are accompanied by simple unfinished projects to familiarize you with the steps. Next dive into the study projects. They illustrate how I use these techniques in my work and how the methods can be layered to achieve more exciting results.

Finally, I hope the quilts shown throughout the book inspire you and increase your confidence. All of the quilts pictured have used at least one, if not all six, of the techniques. I hope that by sharing my inspirations, techniques, and finished pieces, I will encourage you to experiment and find your own artistic style.

Velda E. Newman

Intuitive Design

Look around you. Why did you choose the sweater you're wearing or the chair you're sitting in? Consider what attracts you to your favorite objects and why you chose those items over the countless other choices. Color, shape and texture are powerful forces in our everyday lives. With little effort we surround ourselves with pleasing combinations in our homes, gardens, cars, and clothing. Together these make up our personal sense of style and design. In life, our choices are more intuitive than academic. It's this same intuition that I use in my approach to quilt design.

As I start my design process I almost always begin with color. Few things elicit a more immediate or stirring response. Color can sell a product, elevate a mood, and evoke emotion. It's reassuring to know that with all its power, effective use of color does not require a degree in color theory. Wondrous color is all around us and nature is our greatest teacher. Nature gives us an unlimited palette to work from by creating color combinations often more fabulous than

those made by man. By observing nature you will usually find that the most appealing effects are created by using variations of colors. To obtain realistic results in your quilts you need only study any leaf, butterfly wing, or vegetable skin. You will notice that nature uses many combinations of colors and shades that work together to reveal an even more spectacular whole.

After color I focus on shape. Shapes are the building blocks of design. In my design process the importance of the subject quickly gives way to the individual shapes that make up that subject. As I work, every element of the design is broken down into a shape and given a direction. A flower is nothing more than the sum of its petals, and a fish quickly becomes its components of body, head, fins, and tail. In quiltmaking, the challenge lies in giving a flat piece of fabric three-dimensional characteristics. By determining how the shapes relate to one another in size, volume, perspective, and balance, you can achieve a convincing composition.

mately more satisfying. By incorporating these same elements into your artwork, you can achieve the same satisfying results.

From the dishes in the cupboard to the trees outside, everything has its own unique color, shape, and texture. Becoming an active observer of your surroundings can offer limitless sources from which to draw. Gathering images and objects that interest you is the best way to spark ideas. Every time you see a beautiful ribbon, run across a great magazine photo, or find an autumn leaf you should put it in a book or drawer, or tack these objects up on a special bulletin board where you have constant reminders for sources of inspiration. When composing a quilt, it is exciting to see how a piece of fruit printed on a postcard combines with another image from a tapestry that together sit on a background from a third source. Having such visual aids will help you make decisions, give you alternatives, and focus your energy throughout your creative process.

Whereas shape is recognized only visually, texture is unique in that it stimulates two senses. By appealing to both sight and touch, texture is often an object's most intriguing characteristic. Notice how the chalky outside of a shell is contrasted by its shiny smooth inside. Or consider a brilliant blue tile. Its glaze looks fluid, almost goopy, but it is actually hard and brittle. These types of textural associations make the objects around us richer, more interesting, and ulti-

Materials

Traveler's Tree, 72" x 60", 1998
Techniques used: Shape and Texture
Stitching, Paint, Watercolor Pencil,
Water-soluble Crayon

Each project has its own materials list. In addition you will need the following materials, which I find indispensable. Included are tips on the brands that I like and sources for them.

Sewing Machine

My one and only machine is a Bernina® 910. I still love it after all these years! A zipper foot and a darning or open quilting foot are required for some of the projects. Be kind to your machine; treat it to a thorough cleaning once a year, and insert a new needle each time you begin a new project.

Fabric

Hand-dyed cotton fabrics are used for most of the projects in this book. You can dye your own as I do, or find them readily available at your local quilt shop, in catalogs, or online. Commercial cotton solids that are two-sided are used throughout the projects.

Batting

I use thin cotton batting for most projects. Both Soft Touch® by Fairfield® and the thinnest Dream® batting are good choices.

Pattern Web

I make templates using Pellon Tru-Grid®. It comes 44" wide printed with a 1" blue grid that you can easily see through. Ask for it at your local quilt store.

Fabric Spray Adhesive

This is useful for stabilizing layers of fabric, or for temporary placement of appliqué pieces during the design process. I prefer 505® Spray and Fix, a temporary fabric adhesive.

Lightbox

A lightbox, which is available at most art supply stores, is useful for transferring pattern/template marks or lines to fabric. Taping the fabric to be marked onto a window works just as well in a pinch.

Disappearing Pen

This type of pen marks with ink that disappears on its own. If you purchase a new one, the line lasts about twelve hours.

Iron

A steam iron with a pointed tip at the end is essential.

Hair Dryer

You can use a hair dryer to speed the paint drying process. I keep one in my studio just for this purpose.

Paint

Lots of good textile paints are on the market. Try different brands to see what works best for you. I like Setacolor® by Pebeo®, which is what I used for the pieces throughout this book. The color range is extremely good, they mix easily with water, and are permanent when dry. Lumiere® is a great metallic paint and also has several nice pearlescent colors. The brand Neopaque® covers dark fabric well. Both can be washed or dry-cleaned after heat setting. Dye-na-Flow®, made by Jacquard®, is very thin, almost like dye. You can dilute it even further with water to make lighter values of any color. It comes in thirty colors and is permanent when heat-set with an iron. Any good artist's acrylic paint also works well. They are economical and come in an endless range of colors. These paints are thicker (think toothpaste) than the other choices and require more water to dilute. Artist's acrylic paint is permanent when dry.

Paint Brushes

Choose brushes made expressly for fabric painting or artist's brushes made for acrylic paint. Both have nylon bristles and are stiff enough to force the paint into the weave, thereby bonding the paint to the fabric. Start with 1½" flat and ¾" flat sizes plus a couple of medium-size round brushes. Good (expensive) brushes will last a long time if you take care of them. Always wash brushes with soap and water when you are finished using them.

Mixing Tray

I use an artist's white porcelain tray. Artist's trays also come in plastic. The porcelain ones are much easier to clean and don't absorb paint. It's important to mix on a white surface in order to get a true reading of the colors you are mixing. The trays are available at art supply stores.

Spray Bottle

Use a spray bottle with a trigger handle that produces a fine spray. When the directions call for spraying the fabric with water in preparation for painting, always spray the entire piece. The fabric needs to be evenly wet, but not dripping.

Painting Supplies

When called for in a project, you will need:

- Containers for water
- Containers for paint
- Paper towels
- Paint rags
- Apron
- Plastic dropcloth
- Short clothesline and pins
- Table or other flat surface

Watercolor Pencils, Crayons, and Pastels

Water-soluble colored pencils, crayons, and pastels differ from regular colored pencils, crayons, and pastels in that they mix with water and can be blended like paint. These mediums are important because they can be controlled very easily and in small spaces. I like them especially for accents and shadow lines. Unfortunately, they are not permanent and will fade if the quilt is washed. These products are wonderful for quilts that will not be laundered on a regular basis. Try working with these on a sample piece first. Some good brands to try are Derwent® watercolour pencils, Derwent Aqua Tone® woodless watercolor sticks (made in Switzerland), Stabilo® extra-thick Aquarelle® colored pencils from Germany, or Portfolio® oil pastels made by Crayola®. All of these can be purchased in an art supply store.

Embroidery Hoop

When painting on dry fabric, use an embroidery hoop to keep the fabric taut and prevent it from touching your work surface. For larger pieces you can staple the fabric to a wooden frame.

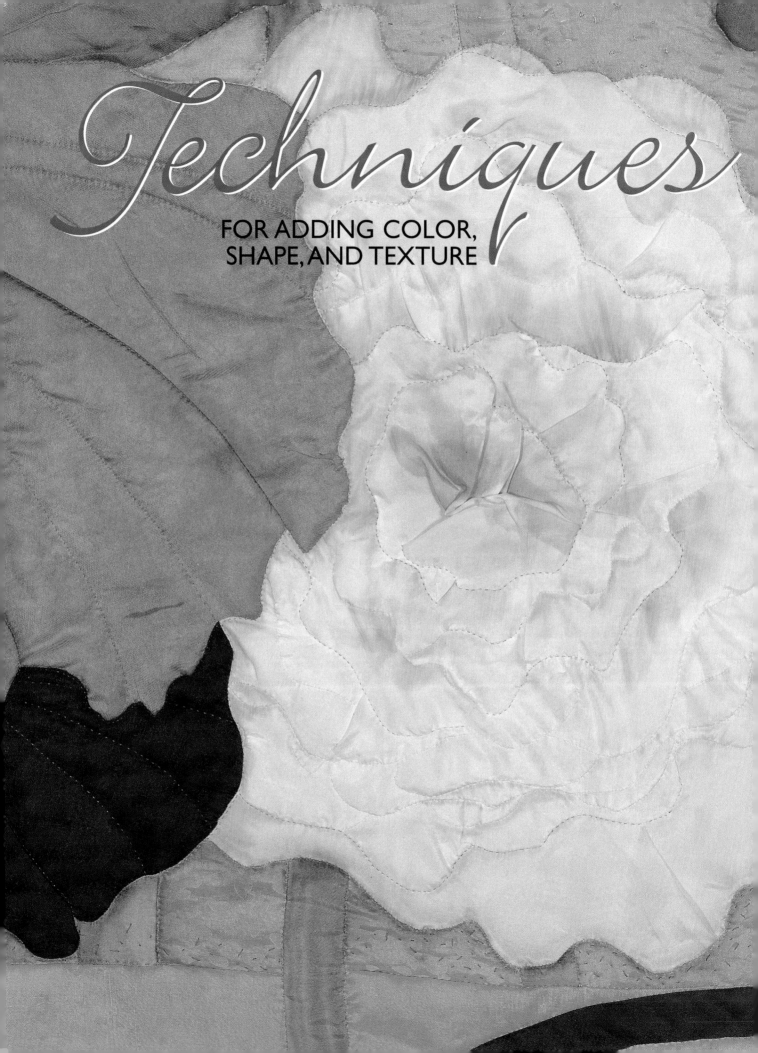

Techniques

FOR ADDING COLOR, SHAPE, AND TEXTURE

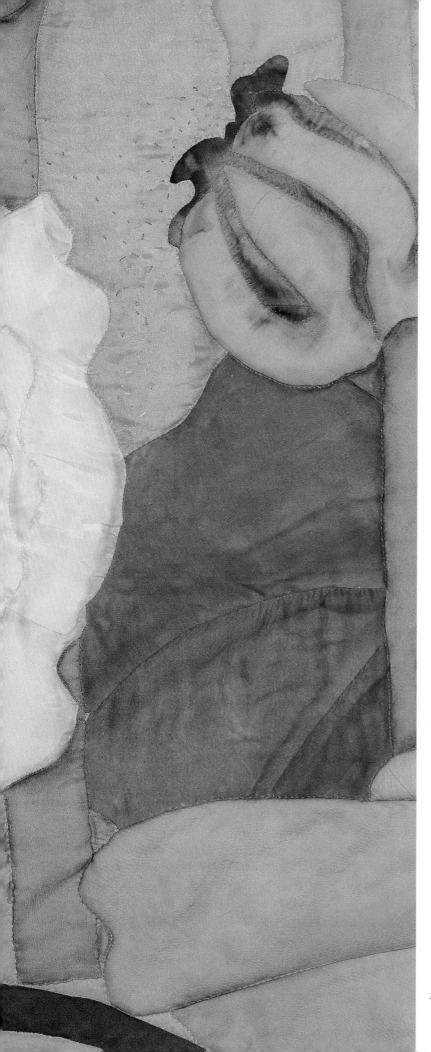

Creating more interesting visual and tactile art remains one of the most exciting aspects of being a quiltmaker. After eighteen years of quilting I have come to rely on the following favorite techniques that are indispensable for conveying color, shape, and texture.

Reverse machine appliqué

Tucks

Shape and texture stitching

Cheesecloth texture

Paint

Watercolor pencil, crayons, and pastels

Some are basic but take just a little practice (tucks technique), while others have been created out of necessity and hours of experimentation (shape and texture stitching).

Begin your exploration by reading through the process for each technique. Some are accompanied with samples—simple unfinished projects to familiarize you with the technique's steps. Next dive into the study projects. They illustrate how I use the shape and texture techniques in my work, and how the methods can be layered to achieve even more exciting results.

Reverse Machine Appliqué Sample

Interesting color patterns and shapes are easily created using reverse machine appliqué. Reverse appliqué involves cutting away the top fabric to reveal layers of fabric underneath. This technique gives you the look of traditional appliqué but in a fraction of the time. It's best to use fabric with a high thread count since it prevents fraying at the point of stitching. Three or four layers of fabric can easily be cut and stitched for a layered appliqué look.

◄Detail of **Hollyhocks** (page 66)

15

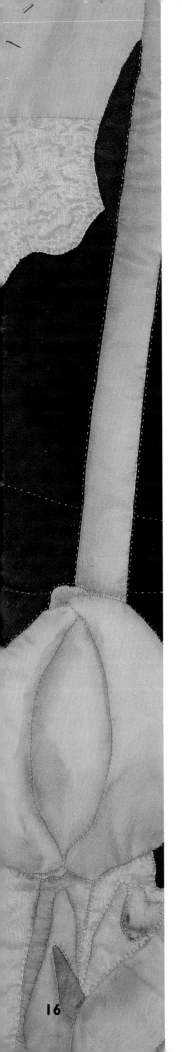

If your shapes can easily be handled with a straight stitch (as in stripes), use a short stitch length setting on your machine and make two rows. If the shape is more complex (rounded objects), install the quilting foot and drop the feed dogs. Using a steady pressure on the foot pedal, move the fabric slowly. It's best to stitch around each shape twice to prevent fraying. Use sharp, pointed scissors for cutting.

Simple Reverse Machine Appliqué

Materials: Three contrasting pieces of fabric

1. Cut the fabrics into 12" squares.

2. Stack the three fabrics with right sides facing up.

3. Draw two lines four inches apart on the top layer.

4. Stitch twice on each line, using short, tight stitches.

5. Cut away the top layer of fabric between the stitching to reveal the second layer. Cut about 1/16" away from the stitching line.

6. Draw two more lines on the newly revealed second layer of fabric, 1" inside and parallel to the first set of lines.

7. Stitch on each line twice, again using short, tight stitches.

8. Cut away the second layer of fabric between the stitching to reveal the third layer.

Tucks

Making tucks is a simple way to create both shape and texture. Depending on how they are used, a different look is produced on the front and back side of the fabric. With the tucks stitched on the front side you get a clean, crisp ridge. Stitching the tucks on the back side of the fabric gives you a pieced look without all the work. What I especially like about incorporating tucks in my pieces is that they give an extra accent line that can be emphasized with paint or pencil.

Many of the quilts in this book contain tucks. Examine the tails and fins of the *Fish Study*.

The tucks in this piece are stitched on the front side to simulate the bony structure of the fish. In the *Tulip Study* the tucks were sewn on the reverse side making it look as if the petals were pieced together.

Match the thread to the top fabric; it will be less visible.

Simple Tucks in All-in-One Piece Leaves

Try this simple exercise for shaping leaves using tucks. These are very fast and easy to make.

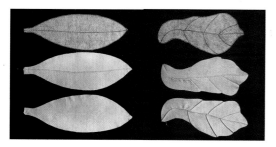

Materials
- ¼ yard green
- ¼ yard pattern web
- Thread to match fabric

Leaf A
1. Cut the template from the pattern web.

2. Cut Leaf A from the green fabric, adding a ¼" seam allowance.

3. Mark a stitching line down the middle of the leaf using a light box and disappearing pen.

4. Fold the fabric on the line and stitch about ¹⁄₁₆" from the folded edge.

Leaf B
1. Cut the template from the pattern web.

2. Cut Leaf B on the bias from the green fabric, adding a ¼" seam allowance.

3. Mark all stitching lines using a light box and disappearing pen.

4. Starting at the outside edge, make the side tucks first by folding the fabric on the line. Stitch a ¹⁄₁₆" tuck, tapering to the middle line.

5. Repeat on the five remaining side tucks.

6. Make the center tuck, enclosing the ends of the side tucks in it.

Basic Rules for Tucks

1. Cut fabric on the bias; use of the bias allows you to make tucks curve or fan outward.

Add contour with tucks.

2. Sew tucks ¹⁄₁₆" from the folded edge of the fabric.

3. Decide how many tucks you are making. Allow approximately ⅛" of fabric for each tuck.

4. For a pieced or softer look, fold and stitch the lines on the wrong side of the fabric.

5. When making a large piece with multiple tucks, always allow extra fabric on all sides of the piece so you can lay the template back on the tucked piece and have plenty of extra room for your seam allowance.

Shape and Texture Stitching

This technique adds the appearance of dimension and shape to a flat piece of fabric. In the process it also adds a wonderful texture. Take a look at the oranges as an example. The secret to achieving proper perspective is in the way the first set of lines are drawn and then stitched. These lines become the guides on which all other stitching is based.

Shape and Texture Stitching Sample

The stem end near the top of the orange was drawn on the fabric first. This is the point at which all curved vertical lines converge. The

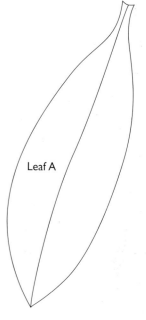

Leaf A

Enlarge 400%.

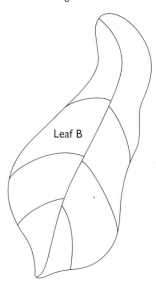

Leaf B

horizontal lines curve up on each end. Notice that they actually form a ring around the stem end near the top. Once your basic lines are drawn, back the fabric shape with thin cotton batting and stitch on each basic line.

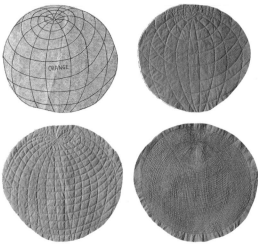

Add shape with stitching.

Materials
- ½ yard orange
- ½ yard thin cotton batting
- Pattern web
- Matching orange thread

Using the oranges as an example, follow these directions for the stitching sequence.

1. Cut the template from the pattern web.

2. Cut the orange from the orange fabric, adding ¼" seam allowance.

3. Cut the orange, without seam allowance, from the batting.

4. Transfer all stitching lines to the orange fabric using a lightbox and disappearing pen.

5. Beginning at the bottom of the orange, stitch on one vertical line to the stem end, pivot and return to the bottom of the orange on the next vertical line over. Stitching in this manner prevents stopping and starting at the stem end, which would result in a lot of cut threads.

6. Repeat the above stitching pattern on all vertical lines.

7. Stitch on all horizontal lines, starting on one side and finishing on the opposite side.

8. Stitch rings around the stem end.

9. When all of the basic lines have been stitched, repeat the stitching pattern, dividing each space in half both horizontally and vertically, using your presser foot as a guide.

10. Repeat the stitching sequence until the lines in the middle are about ¼" apart. The stitching will be much closer together at the top and bottom of the orange because of the curve in the lines.

This technique is used for the *Baskets* quilt (page 43). Only the basic lines were drawn on the fabric and stitched. Some baskets have both horizontal and vertical lines like the oranges, but others have horizontal lines only. Like the orange, all lines are curved to give the basket its rounded form. To exaggerate the shape even further, batting is added and the stitched lines are accented with paint.

This technique can also be used for shapes that aren't circles. The *Traveler's Tree* (page 11), *Sea Shells* (page 56), and *Lemon Study* (page 24) also exhibit this technique.

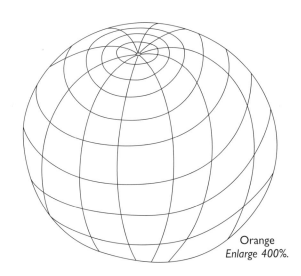

Orange
Enlarge 400%.

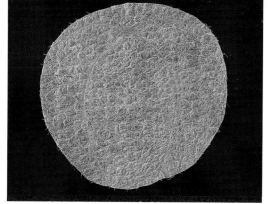

Add texture with pulled threads
and circular stitching

Cheesecloth Texture

Cheesecloth can give a piece great texture and visual appeal. It can be manipulated in so many ways and the results are always interesting. I am constantly asked about the cheesecloth texture in my classes and no one believes me when I tell them how easy it is! I first developed this technique while working on the *Sun Kissed* quilt (page 22). Specifically, I was challenged to find a way to effectively communicate the skin of the melon in the lower left corner. At first, I tried painting and stitching only, but those methods didn't seem to do the melon justice. Finally, venturing out of my studio and into the kitchen I found the answer I was looking for—cheesecloth.

The basic steps for manipulating the cheese-cloth are simple: Layer it with fabric and batting, then stitch them all together on the machine. Try manipulating the cheesecloth in any manner you like. You can cut holes in it, pull some of the threads out, or layer it—the possibilities are endless.

I have a new quilt in mind and I am excited about using this technique for an assortment of farm-fresh vegetables like broccoli and cauliflower. I can also see using it for leaves, the coats of wooly sheep, or on a one-of-a-kind jacket.

Simple Cheesecloth Texture Sample

1. Cut a 12" square of thin cotton batting.

2. Cut a 12" square of fabric.

3. Cut a 14" square of cheesecloth, making sure you cut off any selvage edges.

4. Lay the cheesecloth on a dark surface so the threads are easily seen.

5. Manipulate the cheesecloth in any one or all of these ways:

- Pull some of the threads out horizontally.
- Pull some of the threads out vertically.
- Pull some threads out both horizontally and vertically.
- Layer with other cheesecloth.
- Cut holes in it.
- Paint or dye it.

6. Lay the cheesecloth on top of the fabric and put the batting under the fabric.

7. Spray lightly between the layers with a spray adhesive to hold in place.

8. Using a quilting foot, sew through all three layers. Get creative with your stitching; try different patterns or shapes.

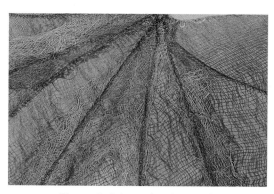

Cheesecloth layered and painted

Paints and Pencils for Dimension and Color

Paints, watercolor pencils, water-soluble crayons, and pastels offer endless opportunities for creating special effects on fabric. Not only do they add color, they also give the illusion of shape, shadow, and form to a flat surface. When I begin a quilt, fabric and composition are my first concern. In the end, however, I depend on paint and pencil work to really bring the piece together and to further draw the viewer's eye around every petal and behind every leaf. To achieve this I draw heavily on my traditional art and painting background. By incorporating other mediums into my work, a realism and depth is achieved that I could not capture using fabric and thread alone. In addition and almost as important, it keeps my design process exciting and dynamic.

Paint

I use paints in two basic ways. One, a transparent wash, is simply created by thinning the paint with a generous amount of water. Once applied, a wash allows some color and properties of the original fabric to show through. Washes are also great for layering to achieve a desired effect without stiffening the fabric. Think of the blush of a peach as it turns from deep yellow to rosy red and all the color nuances in between. Layering washes helps you create this type of realistic color blend.

The second way I use paint is right out of the jar or tube, diluting with only a small amount of water, or none at all. The paint remains close to its original consistency and can be applied to create highlights, shadows, or patterns of color.

Making a Wash with Acrylic Paint

Squeeze or pour a small amount of paint into the mixing tray. With your paintbrush gradually pull water into the paint, thinning so that there are no lumps; it should be the consistency of milk. More paint and less water, which will have a thicker consistency, equals stronger color. Less paint and more water will have a thinner water-like consistency and will yield a weaker color. A good formula to start with is four parts water to one part paint.

Apply the first color to the wet fabric and blend toward the middle.

Apply the second color and blend toward the first color.

To practice with paint on dry fabric, draw or copy a simple sketch. Stretch the fabric in an embroidery hoop so the entire sketch is visible. Mix the paint to the desired consistency: thicker for strong color, thinner for washes and blending. Try several different brushes. Find your style—the more you practice the more comfortable you will become with the medium.

Watercolor Pencils and Water-Soluble Crayons and Pastels

Watercolor pencils and water-soluble crayons and pastels have become indispensable tools for me. They are an easy way to give definition to any part of a design that is lacking by applying additional layers of color, shadow, and contouring. I often find myself weeks after the end of a project going back over areas with colored pencils, crayons, and pastels.

Watercolor Pencil

You can't go wrong with watercolor pencils if you keep in mind one simple rule: Follow a seam line. Accenting a seam with color gives it greater definition. If you want to create a shadow effect on a seam line try choosing a contrasting color. The primary colors red, yellow, and blue are strengthened when paired with their complementary colors green, violet, and orange.

Accenting a Seam Line

Gently push the point of the pencil into the seam line and lay down a line of color.

Next change your hand position and use the side of the pencil to blend the line outward.

Once the color is laid down, soften the line by blending it with a damp cloth or paintbrush. You can also begin with damp fabric and apply color in the same manner as above, then

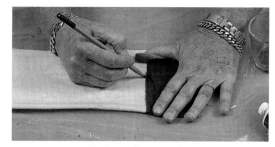
Defining the seam line

Blending the line

To produce more realistic results, always draw on the opposite side of the pressed seam.

smooth with a wet brush. Dry with a hair dryer and press with a hot iron. This helps to set the color. Don't be afraid to experiment!

Water-Soluble Crayons and Pastels

Water-soluble crayons and pastels are great for adding color and additional definition when you don't want to use paint. Use these mediums to fill in, add another layer of color, accentuate highlights, and deepen shadows.

Here are two basic ways to apply crayons and pastels.

Dampen the fabric using a spray bottle. Apply the crayon or pastel, pressing lightly for soft color or harder for more pronounced color. Blend, using a stiff, damp paintbrush. Dry with a hair dryer and press with a hot iron.

Apply the crayon or pastel to dry fabric and blend with a damp cloth. Dry with a hair dryer and press with a hot iron.

I often layer crayon or pastel on top of paint to further enrich the color.

You may find it helpful to practice your painting techniques on paper before attempting them on your project. Remember that porous fabric will draw up thinned paints more rapidly and bleed more than paper does.

▲ *Sun Kissed*, 65" x 168", 1997
Techniques used: Cheesecloth Texture,
Shape and Texture Stitching, Paint,
Watercolor Pencil, Water soluble Crayon

Lemon Study

Techniques Used: Shape and Texture Stitching, Tucks, Paint, and Watercolor Pencil

Everyone loves lemons! Put a few in a bowl and enjoy them for their color, form, and heavenly scent. While working on the large *Sun Kissed* quilt I used the technique of shape and texture stitching to create realistic orange peels. You can also use this technique for grapefruit, limes, and lemons as shown in this study piece. For this composition, buy some lemons and keep them in view as you work. Refer to the real thing as you begin to stitch and paint.

◄ *Lemon Study*, 18" x 19", 2001

Materials

- Lemons: ¼ yard bright yellow
- Leaves: ¼ yard medium green
- Leaves: ¼ yard dull green
- Background: ⅔ yard black and white dot
- Backing: ⅔ yard
- Batting: 20" × 30" thin cotton
- Narrow black piping: 2½ yards
- Thread to match fabrics
- Pattern web
- Acrylic paint–Setacolor® green gold #55
- Watercolor pencil–Derwent® cedar green #50
- Paint supplies (page 13)

Cutting

1. Cut the templates from the pattern web.

2. Cut three lemons from the bright yellow, adding a ¼" seam allowance.

3. Cut five leaves from the medium green using template one. Cut one leaf from medium green using template two, part A. Add ¼" seam allowance to all pieces.

4. Cut four leaves from the dull green using template one. Cut one leaf from the dull green using template two, part B. Add a ¼" seam allowance to all pieces.

5. Cut the branch from the dull green, adding a ¼" seam allowance.

6. Cut three lemons, without a seam allowance, from the batting.

7. Transfer all stitching lines to the three yellow lemons using a lightbox and disappearing pen.

8. Transfer the center tuck line to the wrong side of all template one leaves.

9. Center the batting on the wrong side of each lemon and tack in place with spray adhesive.

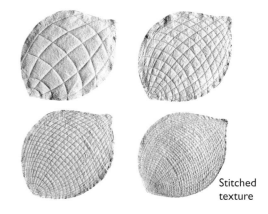

Stitched texture

10. Stitch on all horizontal lines of one lemon using matching thread.

11. Stitch on all vertical lines of the first lemon.

12. Divide each space in half vertically using your presser foot as a guide. Stitch again.

13. Divide each space in half horizontally, using the presser foot as a guide, and stitch again.

14. Repeat this stitching sequence until you have approximately ⅛" between rows of stitching. The lines of stitching will overlap each other at the top and bottom of the lemon.

15. Repeat directions 10–14 for the other two lemons.

16. Place the three stitched lemons in hot water for approximately ten minutes, then dry flat. This will produce a slightly puckered surface.

17. Crease Leaf One on the fold line with right sides together.

18. Stitch a ¹⁄₁₆" tuck with matching thread (page 17). Press to one side. Repeat on all Leaf One leaves.

19. Appliqué piece A to piece B of Leaf Two by hand or machine.

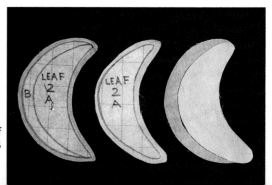

Combining leaf parts A and B

Shadowing is suggested with the use of paint.

Painting

1. Lay lemons on a table and spray with water until damp.

2. Mix one part green gold paint to four parts water.

3. Following the Lemon Study photo, paint the lemons. Notice that the paint is concentrated at the stem end of the upper left lemon. On the bottom center lemon, the paint is applied to the right side, suggesting a shadow from the overlapping right lemon

4. Dry the lemons using a hair dryer.

Quilt Assembly

1. Pin the pieces to the background fabric, referring to the photo and the assembly diagram. Baste.

2. Appliqué the lemons, leaves, and branch using the traditional needle-turn method or machine appliqué.

3. Place the appliquéd piece on top of the batting and baste together.

4. Machine quilt around the lemons, leaves, and branch.

5. Square up the piece to its finished size.

6. With raw edges together, stitch the piping to the right side of the piece at the outer edges, using a zipper foot. Round the corners and overlap the ends.

7. To make a pillowcase lining, place the right sides of the quilted piece and the backing together. Pin the edges.

8. Stitch around the edges using the zipper foot, just inside the stitching for the piping. Leave a 6" opening for turning.

9. Trim the batting, backing, and corners.

10. Turn the piece right side out and slip-stitch the opening closed.

11. Press using a steam iron.

Finishing with Watercolor Pencils

1. Draw a broad line with the side of the green pencil to shade the space between the overlapping lemons (page 21). Blend outward using a damp cloth.

2. Shade the leaves down the center line. Blend outward using a damp cloth (page 21).

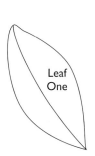

Leaf One

Leaf Two A

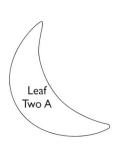

Leaf Two B

Enlarge all patterns 400%.

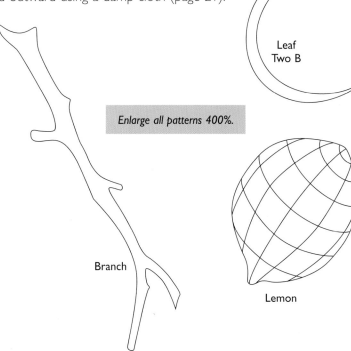

Branch

Lemon

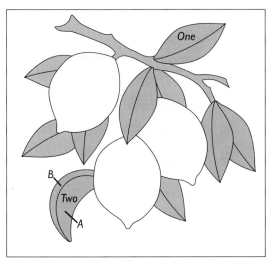

One

B
Two
A

Assembly Diagram for Lemon Study

Melon Study

20" x 36", 2001
Techniques used: Cheesecloth Texture,
Tucks, Paint, Watercolor Pencil,
and Water-soluble Crayon

I brought a few cantaloupes home and put
them in a bowl in the kitchen. Throughout
the next week I observed their shape,
texture, and color.

Although the differences were subtle,
I found each melon I examined to be more
interesting than the last. It's these subtleties,
the unexpected, that I try to convey in my
quilts. It's not hard to train your eye to notice
detail. Once you start designing projects,
capturing the details on the subjects you
choose will give you much more to work
with and make your designs more powerful
than they would be if you used only their
superficial characteristics. The following
technique for melon skin is an idea I came
up with after studying the cantaloupes on
my kitchen sink for a week!

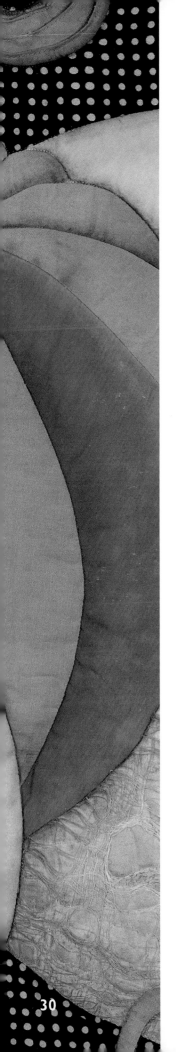

Materials

- Melon One: ⅜ yard pale gold
- Melon Two: ⅓ yard lime green
- Melon Three: ⅓ yard pale yellow, 7" × 12" piece of medium green
- Melon Four: ⅜ yard medium green, 7" × 12" piece of bright orange
- Melons Five and Six: ⅜ yard yellow-green
- Melon Seven: 8" × 12" piece of dark green, 8" × 12" piece of pale yellow
- Leaves and vines: ⅜ yard yellow-green
- Background: ⅔ yard
- Backing: ⅔ yard
- Batting: 1 yard thin cotton
- Cheesecloth: 1 package
- Narrow black piping: 3 yards
- Thread to match fabrics
- Pattern web
- Acrylic paint: Setacolor® raw sienna #25, pernod yellow #18, buttercup #13, moss green #28
- Watercolor pencils: Derwent® mineral green #45, cedar green #50
- Water-soluble crayons: Caran d'Ache® violet, ultramarine, malachite green, yellow-green
- Pencil with eraser
- Paint supplies (page 13)

Melon One

Cutting and Applying Cheesecloth

1. Cut Melon One template from the pattern web.

2. Cut the melon from pale gold fabric, adding ½" seam allowance.

3. Cut the melon, without a seam allowance, from the batting.

4. Cut a square piece of cheesecloth 2" larger that the fabric piece. Cut off any selvages.

5. Lay the cheesecloth on a dark surface to help you see the threads more clearly (page 19).

6. Pull out six horizontal threads every 1" down the entire length of the cheesecloth.

7. Cut six to eight random slits horizontally in the threads.

8. Push the threads back to form larger holes in the cheesecloth, using the eraser end of the pencil. Notice that these holes are horizontal to the melon.

9. Center the batting on the back of the melon.

10. Carefully place the prepared cheesecloth on top of the melon fabric. Tack in place with adhesive spray.

11. Thread your machine with matching thread, install a free-motion quilting foot, and drop the feed dogs.

12. Stitch the layers together, moving in a random horizontal pattern. Curve the stitching to give the melon a rounded appearance.

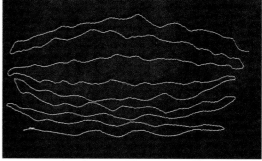

Stitching as seen from the back

Painting

1. Lay the finished melon on the table and spray with water until damp.

2. Mix one part raw sienna paint to four parts water. Apply to the edges of the melon, gradually thinning with more water as you blend the paint in toward the center.

3. Dry with a hair dryer and press. Set aside.

Melon Two

Cutting

1. Cut the melon template from the pattern web.

2. Cut the melon from lime green fabric.

3. Cut Melon Two, without a seam allowance, from the batting.

Painting

1. Lay the melon fabric piece on the table and spray with water until damp.

2. Mix one part moss green paint to two parts water.

3. Apply the paint to the edges of the melon, gradually thinning with more water as you blend the paint in toward the center.

4. Dry with a hair dryer and press. Set aside.

5. Center the batting on back of the melon.

Melon Three

Cutting and Stitching

1. Cut Melon Three and Slice A templates from the pattern web.

2. Cut the melon from the pale yellow fabric, adding ¼" seam allowance on all edges.

3. Transfer all stitching lines to the fabric.

4. Press the seam allowance where the slice is removed to the wrong side of the melon.

5. Cut Slice A from the medium green fabric, adding a generous ½" seam allowance.

6. Lay Slice A on the table and spray with water until damp.

7. Mix one part moss green paint to four parts water.

8. Apply the paint starting from the left side, painting the curved edge and blending toward the middle.

9. Dry with a hair dryer and press.

10. Lay Slice A under the opening of the melon. (The slice is larger than the opening.) Appliqué or topstitch the melon to the slice.

11. Cut the batting ¼" smaller than the melon and center it under the melon.

12. Using lime green thread on top and a regular stitch, sew on the lines. Begin at the bottom of the melon and stitch to the stem end, pivot and return on the same line back to the bottom of the melon.

13. Repeat on all remaining lines.

14. To make the stem end, change to a darning or quilting foot and drop the feed dogs.

15. Outline stitch the circle, which represents the stem end, and spiral the stitching inward. Repeat until the circle is solid with stitching.

Painting

1. Lay the completed melon on the table and spray with water until damp.

2. Mix one part pernod yellow paint to four parts water.

3. Apply the paint to the stitched lines, thinning with water as you blend in toward the middle of each section.

4. Dry with a hair dryer and press. Set aside.

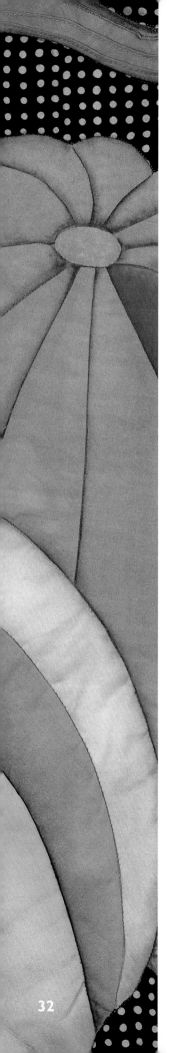

Melon Four

Cutting

1. Cut Melon Four and slice B templates from the pattern web.

2. Cut the melon from the medium green fabric, adding a ¼" seam allowance on all edges.

3. Transfer all stitching lines from the template to the fabric.

4. Press the seam allowance where the slice is removed to the wrong side of the melon.

5. Cut Slice B from the bright orange fabric, adding a ½" seam allowance.

6. Lay Slice B on the table and spray with water until damp.

7. Mix one part moss green paint to four parts water.

8. Paint the curved edge of Slice B, starting from the left side and blending toward the middle.

9. Dry with a hair dryer and press.

10. Insert the slice under the opening in of the melon and appliqué or topstitch in place. Press.

11. Cut the batting ¼" smaller than the finished melon. Center under the melon.

12. Using green thread, stitch on all lines. Begin at the bottom of the melon, stitch to the stem end, pivot and return on the same line back to the bottom of the melon.

13. Repeat on all of the remaining lines.

14. To make the stem end, change to a darning or quilting foot and drop the feed dogs.

15. Outline stitch the circle to represent the stem end. Repeat until the circle is solid with stitching.

Painting

1. Lay the completed melon on the table and spray with water until damp.

2. Mix one part moss green paint to four parts water.

3. Apply paint to the stitched lines, thinning with water as you blend in toward the middle of each section.

4. Dry with a hair dryer and press. Set aside.

Melon Five & Six

Cutting

1. Cut Melon Five and Six templates from the pattern web.

2. Layer the fabric and batting. Cut both melons 1" larger than the templates. This allows you to keep the stitching pattern approximately ½" from the edge.

3. Cut a square of cheesecloth 2" larger than the fabric and batting pieces. Cut off the selvage edges.

4. Lay the cheesecloth on a dark surface to see the threads more clearly.

5. Pull out three threads every 1" horizontally down the entire length of the cheesecloth.

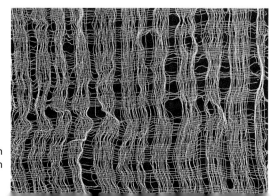

Working with cheesecloth

6. Now pull out three threads every 1" vertically across the width of the cheesecloth until you have a checkerboard pattern.

7. Place the prepared cheesecloth on top of the melon fabric.

8. Push the threads back to produce a circle or hole in the cheesecloth using the eraser end of a pencil. Repeat at all intersections.

9. To produce a more random effect, go back and make smaller circles in the middle of the intersections.

10. Place the cheesecloth on top of the melon fabric. Hold the three layers together with a small amount of spray adhesive.

Stitching

1. Thread the machine with cream-colored thread. Install the quilting foot and drop the feed dogs.

2. Stitch the melon in a random figure-eight motion, loosely following the pattern made by the circles in the cheesecloth. Make small, medium, and large circles this way.

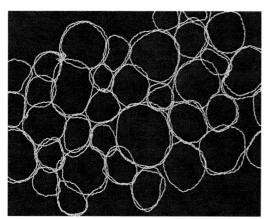

Stitched circles

3. It is easier to start the stitching pattern in the middle of the melon, working toward the outer edge. Keep the stitching approximately ½" from the edge.

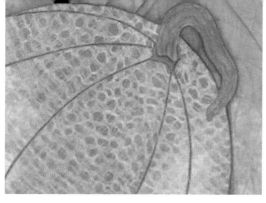

Detail of
Sun Kissed

Finishing

1. Place the template on the finished melon and cut to the correct shape, adding a ¼" seam allowance.

2. Draw a circle for the stem end using the template and a disappearing pen.

3. Change the top thread to dark yellow-green. Using the quilting foot and with the feed dogs down, fill in the circle with solid stitching, moving in a circular motion.

4. Mark the curved stitching lines on the melon following the pattern and using the disappearing pen.

5. Change back to regular stitching. Starting from the bottom of the melon, stitch on the line up to the stem end, pivot and return on the same line. Do this once more on the same line.

6. Repeat on the other three lines.

Melon Seven

Cutting

1. Cut Melon Seven top and bottom templates from the pattern web.

2. Cut the bottom from the dark green fabric, adding a ¼" seam allowance.

3. Cut the top from the pale yellow fabric, adding a ¼" seam allowance.

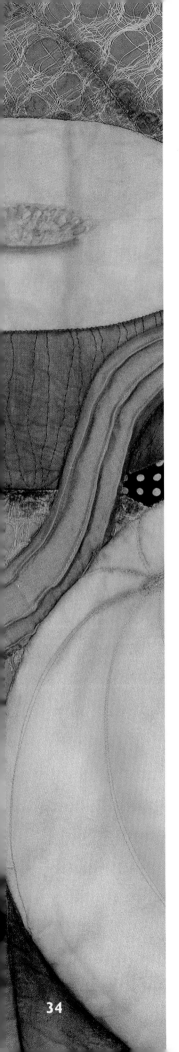

4. Sew the top to the bottom and press the seam allowance toward the green fabric.

5. Mark all stitching lines on the bottom half, and mark the seed cavity on the top half.

6. Cut the batting ¼" smaller than the finished melon. Center it under the melon.

7. Install the darning or quilting foot and drop the feed dogs.

8. Stitch the lines on the bottom half of the melon in a random u-shaped pattern using dark green thread.

Painting

1. Lay the melon on the table. Keep it dry so the paints don't run and bleed.

2. Mix one part buttercup paint to one part water. With a small round brush, make dash marks inside the melon cavity to represent seeds.

3. Dry with a hair dryer.

4. Accent the painted seeds on one side with mineral green watercolor pencil.

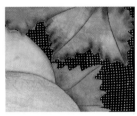

Leaves

Cutting

Note: All three leaves are partial or incomplete units that are inserted into the composition.

1. Cut the Leaf template from the pattern web. Cut the template into eight sections as shown.

2. Cut **one each** of pieces one, two, three, five, and eight from the yellow-green fabric, adding ½" seam allowance. Cut **two each** of pieces four, six, and seven from the same fabric, again adding ½" seam allowance.

3. *Leaf A:* Sew together pieces one, two, three, and four to make half of a leaf (upper right corner of composition).

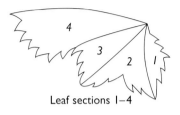

Leaf sections 1–4

4. *Leaf B:* Flip the four pieces over and sew together pieces four, five, six, seven, and eight. Turn this leaf over before placing it in the composition.

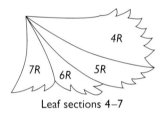

Leaf sections 4–7

5. *Leaf C:* Sew together pieces six, seven, and eight.

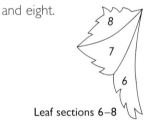

Leaf sections 6–8

Stems

1. Cut Stem templates from the pattern web.

2. Cut two stems on the bias from the yellow-green fabric, adding a ½" seam allowance on all sides.

3. Transfer the tuck lines to the right side of the fabric.

4. Fold the fabric on the tuck line and stitch ¹⁄₁₆" from the folded edge. Repeat on all lines.

5. Press, pulling gently into shape as you go.

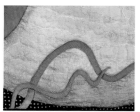

Vines

1. Cut vine templates from the pattern web.

2. Cut the vines from the yellow-green fabric, adding a ¼" seam allowance.

Finishing

1. Pin the pieces to the background fabric referring to the photo and assembly diagram, and baste, turning under the edges. Do not baste the vines to the piece at this time.

2. Appliqué or topstitch melons and stems in place on the background.

3. Thread the machine with green thread. Attach the darning or quilting foot and drop the feed dogs.

4. Stitch leaves using a random, back-and-forth motion to produce a ragged edge.

5. Baste the vines into position and appliqué or topstitch in place.

6. Shade the leaves by applying violet crayon to vein lines and edges. Blend strokes with a damp rag.

7. Shade under Melon Seven and around the edges of Melon Six using the ultramarine crayon. Blend with a damp rag.

8. Shade the contour lines, the stem end, and around the edges of Melon Five with yellow-green crayon.

9. Apply malachite green to Melon Two creating the shadows cast by Melons Four and One. This helps to push Melon Two into the background. Blend all strokes with a damp rag.

10. Apply cedar green pencil to Melon Four to create a shadow cast by Melon Three. Blend all strokes with a damp rag.

Quilt Assembly

1. Steam press the assembled top. Layer the appliquéd piece on top of the batting and baste together.

2. Machine quilt around all melons, leaves, stems, and vines.

3. Square up the piece to the finished size and trim.

4. Stitch the piping using a zipper foot, to the right side of the quilt at the outer edges, rounding the corners and overlapping the ends.

5. To make a pillowcase lining, place the right sides of the quilted piece and the backing together. Pin the edges.

6. Stitch around the edges, just inside the stitching for the piping, leaving a 6" opening for turning.

7. Turn the piece right side out and slipstitch the opening closed.

8. Press well with a steam iron.

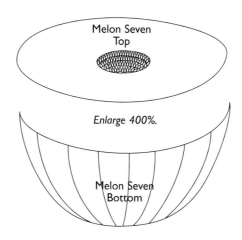

Melon Seven Top

Enlarge 400%.

Melon Seven Bottom

Leaf

1

2

8

3

7

4

6

5

Melon
Two

Vine

Slice
A

Melon
Three

Melon
One

Stem

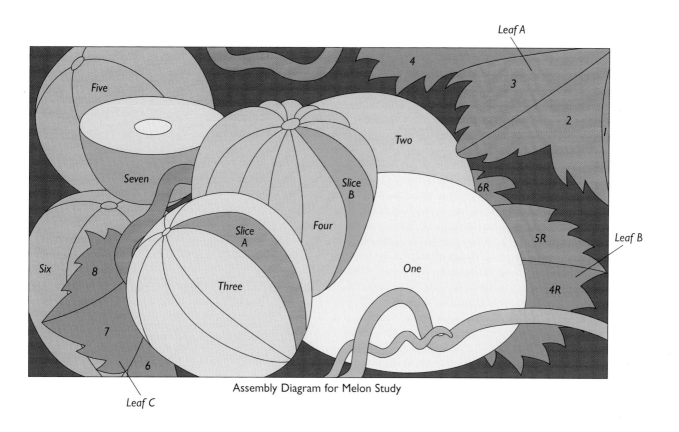

Assembly Diagram for Melon Study

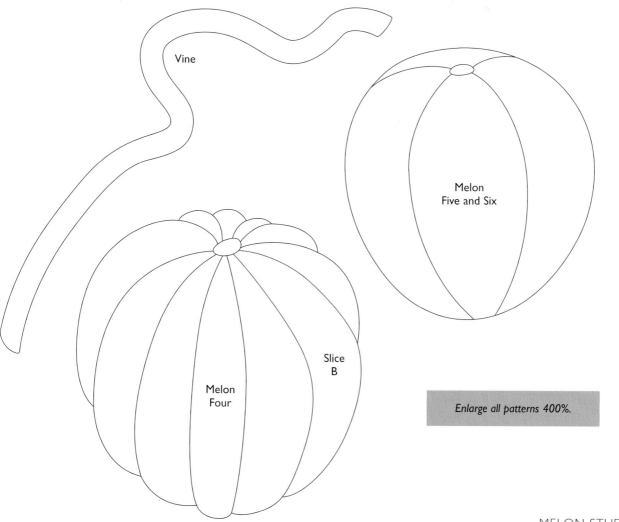

Vine

Melon
Five and Six

Slice
B

Melon
Four

Enlarge all patterns 400%.

Basket

Sample

Techniques used:
Shape, Texture Stitching, and Paint

The *Baskets 1* quilt was inspired by a window
display in an African import store. Of course
the different shapes and sizes were interesting
to me. However, it was the monotone color
scheme and the haphazard way the baskets
were jumbled together that intrigued me
most. I love intense color, and if you're familiar with my work you know that is often the
focus of my pieces. The baskets in the store
window offered a particular challenge to
duplicate in fabric—with little or no color
difference between the various baskets, shape,
shadow, and texture would have to be achieved
by other means. To accomplish this, I used
a simplified version of form and texture
stitching and then exaggerated it with acrylic
paint. I also added texture to the baskets
by using cotton duck, a fabric similar to
canvas. It has a rough, uneven surface and
takes the paint well. Duck is a relatively stiff
fabric, and since hand stitching through it
would be almost impossible I did the entire
piece on the machine. From African baskets,
I changed the focus to American Indian
baskets, a subject more familiar to me.
I relied on a book of American Indian
designs (Dover Books) for pattern ideas
and to get a feeling of how the patterns
naturally wrap around the basket form.

◄ *Baskets 1*, 42" x 44", 1999
Techniques used: Shape and Texture
Stitching, Paint, Watercolor Pencil,
Water-soluble Crayon

The following instructions are for one basket only, the basis for the *Baskets 2* quilt (page 42). Make as many or as few as you want to have in your quilt. Once you have sewn and painted all the basket components everything is simply collaged together and topstitched in place. Notice that this piece has no background or negative space.

Materials for one basket

- ½ yard unbleached cotton duck
- ½ yard thin cotton batting
- 10" square black solid cotton
- Thread to match fabrics
- Pattern web
- Watercolor pencil–Derwent® Vandyke brown #55
- Acrylic paint–Setacolor® raw sienna #25
- Paint supplies (see page 13)

Cutting and Stitching

1. Cut Basket templates A and B from the pattern web.

2. Cut Basket A from the cotton duck, adding a ¼" seam allowance.

3. Cut Basket A, without seam allowance, from the batting.

4. Transfer the stitching lines to the basket using a lightbox and disappearing pen.

5. Cut Piece B, adding a ½" seam allowance, from the black cotton and batting.

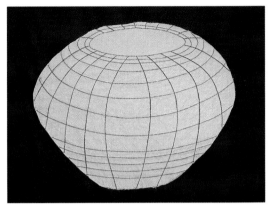

Stitching lines transferred to cotton duck

6. Transfer the stitching lines to Piece B using a lightbox and chalk pencil.

7. Layer Basket A pieces together, centering the batting on the wrong side of the cotton duck.

8. Stitch twice around the "opening" in the basket using brown thread.

9. Starting at the bottom of the basket, stitch each curved, vertical line up to the opening; pivot and return down the same line of stitching.

10. Next, stitch all horizontal lines only once.

Painting

1. Lay the stitched basket on the table and spray with water.

2. Mix one part raw sienna paint with four parts water. Apply color wash.

3. Brush the paint on the basket following the horizontal stitching lines. The paint will be darker at the beginning edge and will lighten as the paint flows around to the other side.

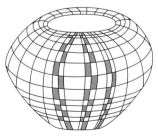

Painting pattern

You will get the best results if you do this very quickly, not worrying about covering every inch with paint.

Color wash added

4. Dry thoroughly with the hair dryer.

5. Accent the contour lines as illustrated. This sample basket was done simply by painting a ½" wide band next to the stitched vertical line, alternating sides where they meet the horizontal lines. Use the brown pencil to draw the lines first, then fill in with paint. You can create your own design but start with something easy for your first basket.

Painting the basket pattern

6. Mix one part raw sienna paint with two parts water. Use this slightly thicker formula to paint the design.

The top of the basket is cut open.

Assembly

1. Cut an opening in the basket leaving a ⅜" seam allowance.

2. Turn the basket over. Trim the batting back to the first row of stitching in the opening to reduce bulk.

3. Clip the seam allowance in the opening to the first stitching line.

4. Press the clipped seam allowance to the wrong side and baste in place.

5. Place black fabric (Piece B) on the batting.

6. Stitch on the stitching lines using black thread.

Try stacking a collection of your own baskets in front of you for inspiration and guidance as you work. When positioning the baskets on your quilt top, pay close attention to how each object relates to and sits on top of another.

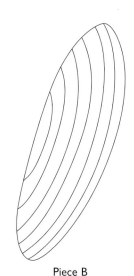

Piece B
Enlarge 400%.

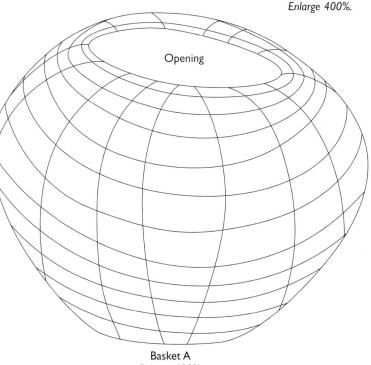

Opening

Basket A
Enlarge 400%.

7. Center the black fabric Piece B under the opening. Baste, then top stitch in place. This represents the inside of the basket as seen from the top.

8. Trim the outside edge of the basket.

9. Turn the seam allowance over the edge of the batting and baste. Press the basket using a steam iron.

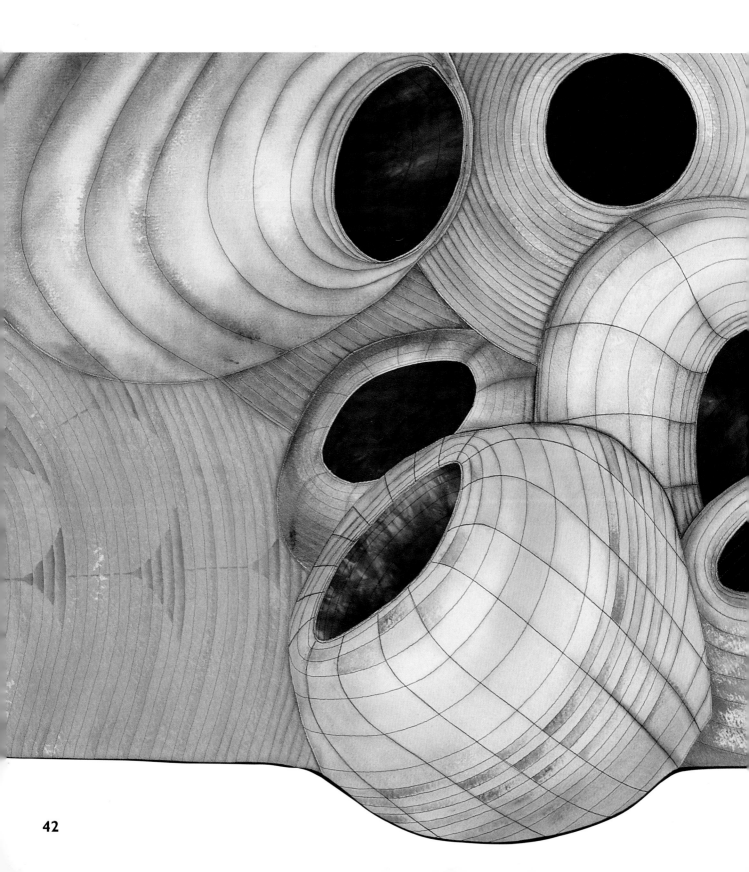

Continue to create as many baskets as you like. Experiment with different sizes, patterns, and colors. Layer and overlap the baskets together and topstitch in place. Notice this piece is made without a background. Any small, leftover spaces between the baskets and around the edges are filled in with pieces that you cut where they overlap on the back side.

▲ *Baskets 2*, 28" × 59", 2001
Techniques used: Shape and Texture
Stitching, Paint, Watercolor Pencil,
Water-soluble Crayon

Shell Study

23" x 38", 2001
Techniques used: Machine Reverse Appliqué,
Paint, Watercolor Pencil, Tucks,
Shape and Texture Stitching

I grew up in southern California where my favorite memories are of the beach. My brothers, sister, and I spent lots of time hunting and collecting shells, competing to find the largest, most colorful, and most unique. Years later, when my children were young, they played the same game.

Materials

- Hand-dyed fabrics work best for this study.
- Shell One: 1/3 yard pale gold
- Shell Two: 1/2 yard peach, 1/2 yard orange, 1/2 yard medium brown
- Shell Three: 1/4 yard white
- Shell Four: 1/4 yard yellow
- Shell Five: 1/4 yard white, 1/4 yard dark brown
- Shell Six: 1/4 yard white, 1/4 yard dark brown
- Shell Seven: 1/3 yard gray
- Shell Eight: 1/3 yard dark gray
- Shell Nine: 1/4 yard burnt orange
- Shell Ten: 1/4 yard white, 1/4 yard dark brown
- Shell Eleven: 1/4 yard dark gold
- Shell Twelve: 1/3 yard white
- Shell Thirteen: 1/4 yard white, 1/4 yard dark brown
- Backing: 3/4 yards
- Batting: 1 yard thin cotton
- Narrow tan or black piping: 3 yards
- Pattern web
- Thread to match fabrics
- Monofilament thread
- Acrylic paints: Setacolor® raw sienna #25, vermilion #26, cobalt blue #11, ultramarine #12, Bengal pink #22
- Watercolor pencil—terracotta #64, light violet #26, jade green #41
- Paint supplies (page 13)

Shell One

Cutting and Stitching

1. Cut the template (page 55) from the pattern web.

2. Cut the shell from the pale gold fabric, adding a 1/4 seam allowance.

3. Cut the shell from the batting without seam allowance.

4. Transfer the stitching line to the right side of the fabric using a lightbox and disappearing pen.

5. Center the batting on the back of the shell.

6. Sew along the marked line starting at the outside edge. At the end of the spiral, pivot and stitch back to the outside edge next to the first line of stitching.

Painting

1. Lay the shell on the table and spray with water until damp.

2. Mix one part raw sienna paint to four parts water.

3. With a small, round brush paint along the stitched line blending outward.

4. Dry with a hair dryer and press.

Finishing

Turn the seam allowance over the edge of the batting and baste.

Shell Two

Cutting and Stitching

Make three different shells using this pattern.

1. Cut the template for Shell Two (page 53), and parts A and B, from the pattern web.

2. Cut three shells (one from each fabric) on the bias, leaving a generous 1/2" seam allowance.

3. Cut pieces A and B from each fabric to match the shell bodies, leaving a 1/4" seam allowance.

4. Transfer stitching lines to the **wrong** side of the fabric.

5. Fold the fabric on the first line and sew, making a 1/16" tuck. Sew all remaining lines in the same manner.

6. Sew pieces A and B to the sides of the appropriate shells.

7. Iron the three stitched shells, gently pulling them into shape as you go.

8. Lay the template back on the shells and trim, leaving a 1/4" seam allowance.

Painting

1. Lay the peach and orange shells on the table and spray with water until damp.

2. Mix one part raw sienna paint to four parts water.

3. Paint on all tuck and seam lines with a small brush, blending outward.

4. Dry with a hair dryer and press.

5. Lay the brown shell on the table and spray with water until damp.

6. Apply jade green pencil on all of the tucks and seam lines blending outward (page 20).

7. Dry with a hair dryer and press.

Finishing

1. Lay the finished shells on the batting.

2. Cut the batting 1/4" smaller than the finished shells. Center it under the shells.

3. Turn the seam allowance over the edge of the batting and baste.

Shell Three

Cutting and Stitching

1. Cut the template (page 53) from the pattern web.

2. Cut Shell Three from the white fabric, adding a 1/4" seam allowance.

3. Cut Shell Three from the batting without a seam allowance.

4. Transfer all stitching lines to the right side of the fabric.

5. Center the batting on the wrong side of the fabric, and tack it in place with spray adhesive.

6. Stitch on each marked line using tan thread.

Painting

1. Lay the shell on the table and spray with water until damp.

2. Mix one part vermilion paint to six parts water.

3. Paint along the stitching lines and around the edges, thinning with water as you blend toward the middle.

4. Dry with a hair dryer and press.

Finishing

Turn the seam allowance over the edge of the batting and baste.

Shell Four

Cutting and Stitching

1. Cut the template (page 53) from the pattern web.

2. Cut Shell Four from the yellow fabric, adding a ¼" seam allowance.

3. Cut Shell Four from the batting without seam allowance.

4. Transfer all stitching lines to the right side of the fabric.

5. Center the batting on the wrong side of the fabric and tack it in place with spray adhesive.

6. Sew along the marked line starting at the outside edge. At the end of the spiral, pivot, and stitch back to the outside edge next to the first line of stitching.

Using Watercolor Pencil

1. Lay the shell on the table and spray with water until damp.

2. Shade along the stitching lines using the light violet pencil and blending outward.

3. Dry with a hair dryer and press.

Finishing

Turn the seam allowance over the edge of the batting and baste.

Shell Five

Cutting and Stitching

1. Cut the templates (page 54) from the pattern web.

2. Cut pieces A and B from the white fabric, adding a ¼" seam allowance.

3. Transfer all markings.

4. Cut one piece A from the dark brown fabric without a seam allowance.

5. Center the dark brown piece A under the white piece A.

6. Install a quilting foot and drop the feed dogs.

7. Stitch twice around all irregular squares using white thread.

8. Trim the white fabric to the stitching line on the inside of each square. Be careful not to cut the brown fabric underneath.

9. Turn the piece over and trim the dark brown fabric between the squares, leaving a ¼" seam allowance.

Painting

1. Lay pieces A and B on the table and spray with water until damp.

2. Mix ½ part Bengal pink and ½ part raw sienna paint to six parts water.

3. Paint along the outside edges of piece A, thinning with more water as you blend toward the middle of the shell.

4. Paint along the inside edge of piece B where it will join piece A, thinning with more water as you blend toward the outside edge.

5. Dry with a hair dryer and press.

Finishing

1. Stitch piece A to piece B. Press the seam allowance toward piece A.

2. Lay the finished shell on the batting.

3. Cut the batting ¼" smaller than the finished shell.

4. Turn the seam allowance over the edge of the batting and baste.

5. Using white thread, stitch twice on each stitching line at the top of the shell.

6. Apply terracotta pencil along the stitched lines at the top of the shell and where piece A and B join (page 20). Blend pencil with a damp rag.

Shell Six

Cutting and Stitching

Note: Shell Six is cut into two pieces in the composition.

1. Cut the template (page 54) from the pattern web.

2. Lay the dark brown fabric on the white fabric, right sides up.

3. Pin the template on top of the fabrics and cut, adding a ¼" seam allowance.

4. Cut Shell Six from the batting without a seam allowance.

5. Separate the two fabric shells.

6. Transfer all markings with a chalk pencil to the right side of the brown shell only.

7. Place the white shell underneath the brown shell, matching the edges.

8. Install the quilting foot and drop the feed dogs.

9. Stitch twice around all irregular circles, using dark brown thread.

10. Trim the brown fabric inside the circles, close to the stitching. Be careful not to cut the white fabric underneath.

11. Turn the shell over. Trim the white fabric around the circles, leaving a ¼" seam allowance next to the stitching.

12. Center the batting on the back of the shell.

13. Stitch twice on each curved line at the top of the shell.

Painting

1. Lay the shell on the table and spray with water until damp.

2. Mix one part raw sienna paint to four parts water.

3. Paint the bottom half only of each of the white shapes using a small brush, blending upward from the bottom.

4. Dry with a hair dryer and press.

Finishing

Turn the seam allowance over the edge of the batting and baste.

Shell Seven

Cutting and Stitching

Note: This shell is used as a filler. Cut it in several pieces to fill in the edges of the quilt.

1. Cut the template (page 55) from the pattern web.

2. Cut Shell Seven from the gray fabric, adding a ¼" seam allowance.

3. Transfer all stitching lines to the right side of the fabric.

4. Cut Shell Seven from the batting without a seam allowance.

5. Center the batting on the back of the shell.

6. Sew on all lines.

Painting

1. Lay the shell on the table and spray with water until damp.

2. Mix one part cobalt blue paint to four parts water.

3. Paint along the stitching lines blending with water as you go.

4. Dry with a hair dryer and press.

Finishing

Turn the seam allowance over the edge of the batting and baste.

Shell Eight

Cutting and Stitching

1. Cut the template (page 55) from the pattern web.

2. Cut Shell Eight from the dark gray fabric, adding a ¼" seam allowance.

3. Cut Shell Eight from the batting without a seam allowance.

4. Transfer the stitching line to the right side of the gray fabric.

5. Center the batting on the wrong side of the shell.

6. Stitch along the marked line starting from the outside edge. At the end of the spiral,

pivot and stitch back to the outside edge along the first line of stitching.

Painting

1. Lay the shell on the table and spray with water until damp.

2. Mix one part raw sienna paint to three parts water.

3. Paint on stitching lines with a small brush and blend outward.

4. Dry with a hair dryer and press.

Finishing

Turn the seam allowance over the edge of the batting and baste.

Shell Nine

Cutting and Stitching

1. Cut the template (page 54) from the pattern web.

2. Separate the template into eight sections—A, B, C, D, E, F, G, and H.

3. Cut the eight sections on the bias from the orange fabric, adding a ½" seam allowance to pieces D, F, G for tucks. Add ¼" seam allowance to remaining pieces.

4. Transfer the tucking lines to the right sides of fabric pieces D, F, and G.

5. Fold piece D on the first line and make a ⅛₆" tuck. Repeat on the next two lines. Do the same for pieces F and G.

6. Sew piece A to B and piece B to C starting at the top of the shell.

7. Sew piece C to D, piece D to E, piece E to F, piece F to G, and piece G to H.

8. Press all seams toward the bottom of the shell.

Painting

1. Lay the shell on the table and spray with water until damp.

2. Mix one part ultramarine paint to four parts water.

3. Paint along the seam lines, working the paint into the tucks and thinning with water as you blend outward.

4. Dry with a hair dryer and press.

Finishing

1. Cut the batting ¼" smaller than the finished shell and center on the wrong side of the shell.

2. Turn the seam allowance over the edge of the batting and baste.

Shell Ten

Cutting and Stitching

1. Cut the template (page 55) from the pattern web.

2. Stack the dark brown fabric on the white fabric, right sides up.

3. Pin the template to the fabric sandwich and cut, adding a ¼" seam allowance.

4. Cut Shell Ten from the batting without a seam allowance.

5. Separate the two fabric shells.

6. Transfer all stitching lines to the right side of the white shell.

7. Return the brown shell underneath, matching edges.

8. Stitch on each marked line twice using white thread.

9. Trim the white fabric (rows marked with an x) close to stitching lines to reveal the brown fabric underneath.

10. Turn the shell over and cut away the brown fabric, leaving a ¼" seam allowance under the white stripes.

Painting

1. Lay the shell on the table and spray with water until damp.

2. Mix one part raw sienna paint to four parts water.

3. Paint around the outside edges, thinning with water as you blend toward the middle.

4. Dry with a hair dryer and press.

Finishing

1. Center batting on the back of the shell.

2. Turn the seam allowance over the edge of the batting and baste.

Shell Eleven

Cutting and Stitching

1. Cut the template (page 54) from the pattern web.

2. Cut Shell Eleven from the dark gold fabric, adding a ¼" seam allowance.

3. Cut Shell Eleven from the batting without a seam allowance.

4. Transfer stitching lines to the right side of the dark gold fabric using a lightbox and disappearing pen.

5. Center the batting on the wrong side of the fabric. Starting at the outside edge sew on the marked line. At the end of the spiral, pivot and stitch back to the outside edge, next to the first line of stitching.

Using Watercolor Pencil

1. Lay the shell on the table and spray with water until damp.

2. Using light violet pencil shade along stitched lines, blending outward with a damp rag or small brush.

3. Dry with a hair dryer and press.

Finishing

Turn the seam allowance over the edge of the batting and baste.

Cutting and Stitching

1. Cut the template (page 54) from the pattern web.

2. Cut Shell Twelve from the white fabric, adding a ¼" seam allowance.

3. Cut Shell Twelve from the batting without seam allowance.

4. Transfer stitching lines to the right side of the white fabric using a lightbox and disappearing pen.

5. Center the batting on the back of the shell.

6. Sew on all curved lines once with tan thread.

Painting

1. Lay the shell on the table and spray with water until damp.

2. Mix one part Bengal pink paint to six parts water.

3. Paint along stitching lines blending with water as you go.

4. Dry with a hair dryer and press.

Finishing

Turn the seam allowance over the edge of the batting and baste.

Cutting and Stitching

1. Cut the template (page 54) from the pattern web.

2. Stack the dark brown fabric and white fabric together, right sides facing up.

3. Pin the template to the fabric sandwich and cut Shell Thirteen, adding a ¼" seam allowance.

4. Cut Shell Thirteen from the batting without a seam allowance.

5. Separate the two fabric shells.

6. Transfer all stitching lines to the right side of the white shell.

7. Place the brown shell under the white shell, matching the edges.

8. Stitch on all stitching lines twice using white thread.

9. Trim the white fabric (rows marked with x) close to the stitching lines to reveal the brown fabric underneath.

10. Turn the shell over and trim the brown fabric, leaving a ¼" seam allowance under the white stripes.

Painting

1. Lay the shell on the table and spray with water until damp.

2. Mix one part burnt sienna paint to four parts water.

3. Paint around the outside edges, thinning with water as you blend toward the middle.

4. Dry with a hair dryer and press.

Finishing

1. Center the batting on the back of the shell.

2. Turn the seam allowance over the edge of the batting and baste.

Quilt Assembly

This study is assembled collage style similar to the Basket study (page 38). Its size is determined by the size of your shells and the need to fill in spaces where shells do not naturally overlap. Use the grid of your cutting mat as a guide when arranging your finished shells into any pattern you please. Pin together and baste. The partial shells are cut from the back of the quilt where one shell overlaps another. Cut these pieces as you baste the quilt together, and add the cut pieces to fill in spaces and make straight edges. You could also make a few extra shells for this purpose.

1. Baste the finished shells together.

2. Thread the top of the machine with monofilament thread.

3. Stitch very close to the edge on all shells. Remember to cut away partial shells underneath and add them to the outside edges.

4. Turn the piece over and trim any remaining excess shells, leaving a ¼" seam allowance.

5. Press and trim to size.

6. Machine baste the piping to the right side of the quilt at the outer edges, rounding the corners and overlapping the ends.

7. To make a pillowcase lining, place the right sides of the quilt and backing together. Pin the edges.

8. Sew around the edges, just inside the stitching for the piping, leaving a 6" opening for turning.

9. Trim the batting, backing, and corners.

10. Turn the quilt right side out and slipstitch the opening closed.

11. Press well using steam.

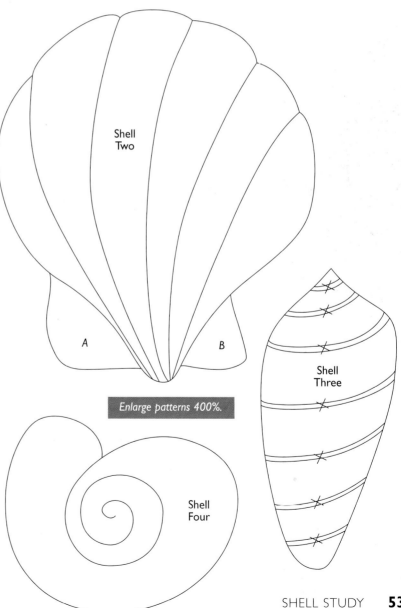

Shell Two

A

B

Enlarge patterns 400%.

Shell Three

Shell Four

A

B

C

D

Enlarge all patterns 400%.

Shell Twelve

E

Shell Nine

F

G

H

Shell Six

Shell Five

B

A

Shell Eleven

54

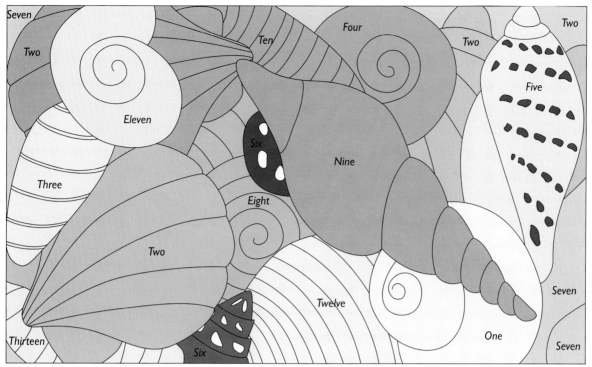

Assembly Diagram for Shell Study

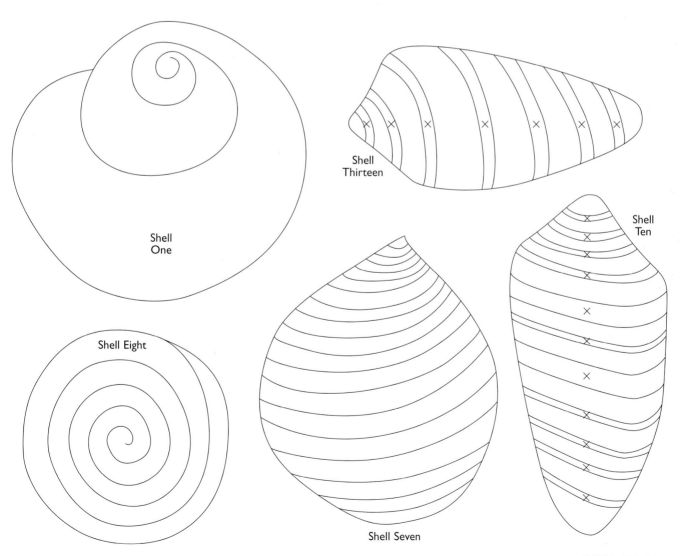

Shell
One

Shell
Thirteen

Shell
Ten

Shell Eight

Shell Seven

Sea Shells, 50" x 144", 2002
Techniques used: Reverse Machine Appliqué,
Shape and Texture Stitching, Tucks, Paint,
Watercolor Pencil, Water-soluble Crayon

Tulip Study

Techniques used: Tucks,
Paint, and Watercolor Pencil

Flowers have always been one of my
favorite subjects for quilts. The combination
of colors, shapes, and sizes are unbeatable
for exciting compositions. I like to work
with simple flowers—those that I remember
in my grandmother's garden and those we
all know and love such as geraniums, iris,
nasturtiums, tulips, and hollyhocks. When
working on flower pieces I surround myself
with the real thing. The inspiration for the
Tulip Study came from a big bunch of early
spring flowers. The bouquet contained many
blossoms but the tulips stole the show.
Included in this lesson are directions for
"paint dipping." Paint dipping is an easy
way to apply paint without using a brush.
It can be used for just about any kind of
flower petal.

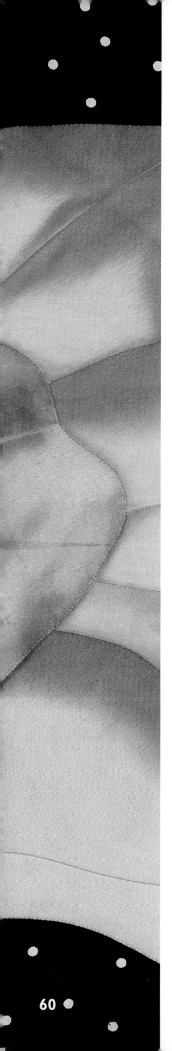

Materials

- Tulip: ¼ yard bright yellow solid
- Stems: ½ yard medium green solid
- Background: ½ yard black and white dot
- Backing: ½ yard
- Batting: ½ yard thin cotton
- Narrow black piping: 2½ yards
- Thread to match fabrics
- Pattern web
- Acrylic paint: Setacolor® vermilion red #26
- Watercolor pencil: Derwent® magenta #22
- Paint supplies (page 13)

Cutting and Making Tucks

1. Cut the petal templates from the pattern web.

2. Cut all of the tulip petals from the solid yellow fabric, adding a ¼" seam allowance.

3. Cut a 1" × 24" bias strip from the medium green solid for the stems.

4. Transfer the center tuck line to the wrong side of the petals using a lightbox and a disappearing pen.

5. Fold each petal on the center tuck line and stitch a 1/16" tuck.

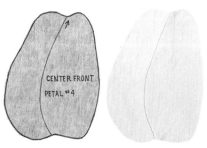

Crease each petal on the fold line
and stitch to create the tuck.

6. Press all tucks to one side.

7. Fold the stem bias strips in half with wrong sides together.

8. Stitch a ⅛" seam down the raw edge.

9. Fold the seam to the back of the stem and press.

Painting the Flower Petals

1. Lay the stitched petals on a table and spray with water until damp.

2. Mix one part vermilion paint to four parts water.

3. Dip the edge of the petal into the paint as shown. The petal should be upside down as you dip.

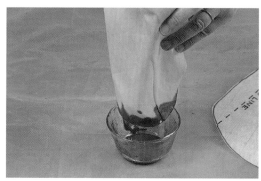

Dip the edge of the petal into the paint.

4. Grab the painted edge and turn the petal in the opposite direction—this is messy but fun!

5. Watch closely as the paint "bleeds" into the wet fabric.

Petal with painted edge

6. When it reaches the point where you wish to stop the bleed turn the petal back to the starting position.

7. Pin the petal to a clothesline with straight pins to air dry. Place a plastic drop cloth under the petals to catch paint drips.

Hang the petals to dry.

8. Continue this painting technique with the rest of the petals and hang them on the clothesline to dry.

Finishing

1. Fold Petal Two on the fold line with right sides together and press. Clip ¼" on the outside edge at the fold line and appliqué in place.

Clip on the fold line.

2. Cut the stems from the bias strip and pin all of the pieces to the background fabric (see Assembly Diagram). Baste in place.

3. Appliqué in place.

4. Turn the piece over and trim the background fabric from behind the petals, leaving a ¼" seam allowance.

5. Center the batting on the wrong side and machine quilt around the petals and stems.

6. Square up the piece to the finished size and press.

7. Using a zipper foot, match raw edges and stitch the piping to the right side of the piece at the outer edges, rounding the corners and overlapping the ends.

8. To make a pillowcase lining, place the quilted piece and backing right sides together.

9. Stitch around the edges just inside the stitching for the piping. Leave a 6" opening for turning right side out.

10. Trim the batting, backing, and corners.

11. Turn the piece right side out and slipstitch the opening closed.

12. Press using a steam iron.

Using Watercolor Pencil

To add definition, shade between the petals using the magenta watercolor pencil (page 21) and blend outward using a damp cloth.

For larger petals or pieces of fabric, start by pinning the cut shapes to the clothesline in the "up" position. Using a brush, apply the paint to the hanging shapes and watch the paint bleed. Once the desired effect is achieved simply remove from the clothesline and re-pin in the "down" position. Let the pieces air dry.

NOTE: Patterns for Tulip are on page 65.

Hollyhock Sample

Techniques used: Tucks, Paint, Watercolor Pencil, Water-soluble Crayon

The rich colors of hollyhocks in my garden inspired the quilt on pages 66-67. The techniques used to create *Hollyhocks* are similar to those used for the *Tulip Study*.

◄ Detail of *Hollyhocks*, 62" x 106", 2001

Materials for One Flower

- Flower: ⅜ yard bright yellow solid
- Center: 3" square yellow-green solid
- Background: 32" square medium value
- Batting: 32" square thin cotton
- 30" square backing
- Narrow piping: 3½ yards
- Acrylic paint: Setacolor® vermilion #26
- 1½" paintbrush
- Thread to match fabrics
- Paint supplies (see page 13)

Cutting

1. Cut the templates from the pattern web, then cut the flower into six sections.

2. Cut pieces 1-6 from the bright yellow fabric, adding ¼" seam allowance.

3. Cut piece 7 from the small piece of yellow-green fabric, adding a ¼" seam allowance.

Sewing and Painting

1. Sew pieces 4, 5, and 6 together and set aside.

2. Sew pieces 1, 2, and 3 together.

3. Lay this unit on the table and spray with water until damp.

4. Mix one part vermilion paint to four parts water.

5. Apply paint starting in the middle and blending toward the outer edge.

6. Dry all pieces with a hair dryer. Press seams toward the middle.

Assembly

1. Hand appliqué piece 7 in place on the lower part of the flower (1, 2, and 3).

2. Sew the two halves of the hollyhock together. Press the seam up.

Finishing

You can make more of these flowers and create your own hollyhock study, or you can finish this single flower as a small quilt.

1. Baste the flower to the background adding stems and buds to make a pleasing composition.

2. Appliqué all pieces in place with needle-turn or machine appliqué.

3. Place the piece on the batting and baste.

4. Machine or hand quilt. Square up the piece to 30".

5. Apply the piping to the right side of the quilt, raw edges together, using a zipper foot.

6. To make a pillowcase lining, place right sides of the quilt and the backing together. Pin the edges.

7. Sew around the edges just inside the stitching line for the piping, leaving a 6" opening for turning. Trim.

8. Turn and press with a steam iron. Slipstitch the opening closed.

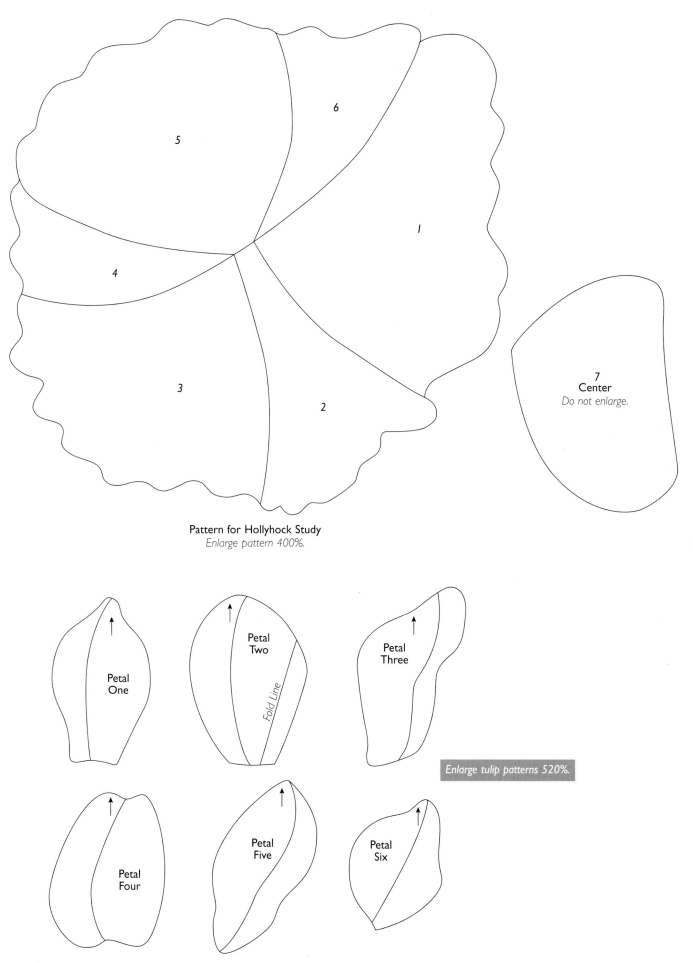

5

6

4

1

3

2

7
Center
Do not enlarge.

Pattern for Hollyhock Study
Enlarge pattern 400%.

Petal
One

Petal
Two

Fold Line

Petal
Three

Enlarge tulip patterns 520%.

Petal
Four

Petal
Five

Petal
Six

▲ *Hollyhocks,* 62" x 106", 2001
Techniques used: Tucks, Paint,
Watercolor Pencil, Water-soluble Crayon

Trout Study

42" x 68", 2001
Techniques used: Tucks, Paint,
Watercolor Pencil

In 1998 I was asked to participate in the *Women of Taste* exhibit. Its purpose was to raise money for Girls Incorporated, a non-profit organization celebrating its twentieth anniversary. The quilts for the exhibit were to be based on and inspired by the lives of women chefs. I was paired with Elizabeth Terry, a wonderful chef and the proprietor of Elizabeth on 37th in Savannah, Georgia. I spent some time with Elizabeth in and around Savannah and at her restaurant, and I was inspired by her passion for sport fishing and the incredible seafood she serves. Who ever knew fish were so interesting? *Catch of the Day* (page 76) was the first quilt I made featuring fish and since then I have made several more.

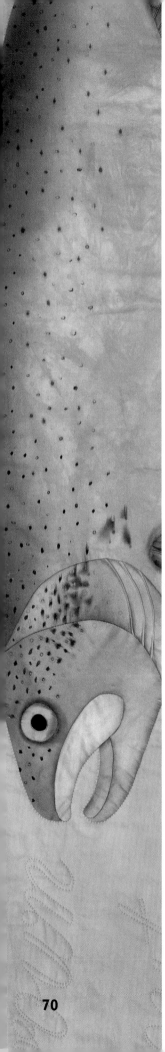

Materials

- Fish: 1⅓ yards white
- Fins: ⅔ yard yellow
- Eye: 4" square black
- Eye: 4" square yellow
- Backing: 2 yards
- Background: 2 yards
- Batting: 2 yards thin cotton
- Pattern web
- Thread to match fabrics
- Acrylic paint: Setacolor® green-gold #55, raw sienna #25, vermilion #26, lemon yellow #17
- Watercolor pencil: Derwent® copper beech #61
- Permanent markers: black, red, yellow
- Color resist (Delta® brand) for fabrics
- 1½" paintbrush
- Paint supplies (see page 13)

Golden Trout

Cutting

1. Cut the templates (1-13) from the pattern web.

2. Cut piece 12 (eye) from the black fabric, adding a ⅛" seam allowance.

3. Cut piece 13 (eye) from the small piece of yellow fabric, adding a ⅛" seam allowance.

4. Cut pieces 1 (body), 3 (fin), 9 (head), 10 (upper lip), and 11 (lower lip) from the white fabric, adding ¼" seam allowances.

5. Cut pieces 2, 4, 5, 7 (fins), and 8 (gills) from the white fabric, adding ½" seam allowances.

6. Transfer the lines for the tucks to the right side of the fabric for these fins and gills.

7. Cut piece 6 (tail). Place the pattern on the bias on the white fabric, allowing 2" seam allowance on all sides. Transfer the lines for the tucks. Stitch 1/16" tucks.

8. For pieces 2, 4, 5, 7 and 8 fold the fabric on the marked lines and stitch 1/16" tucks.

9. Press the fins and gills flat, gently pulling them into shape as you press.

10. Lay the corresponding pattern pieces back on the tucked fabric pieces and trim leaving a ⅛" seam allowance.

Painting

Three colors were used to paint the body of the fish. The lower part is painted with vermilion, and the upper part is painted with green-gold. Raw sienna was used to add large spots across the middle. You will need three containers to mix the paints.

1. Lay all the pieces with the exception of 12 and 13 on the table and spray with water until damp.

2. Place a small amount of vermilion paint in one paint tray, green-gold in another, and raw sienna in the third. Add approximately four parts water to one part paint in each container and mix until each color is quite thin.

3. Paint the green-gold in one stroke across the body with a 1½" brush starting at the top upper edge.

Paint the top edge in one stroke.

4. Immediately dip your brush in water and blot on a paper towel. Brush across the bottom edge of freshly applied green-gold paint, blending toward the center of the body. Paint should blend from dark at the top to light toward the center. Rinse the brush.

5. Apply vermilion paint in the same way starting from the bottom outside edge of the fish. Paint should blend from dark at the bottom to light toward the center. The two colors should be very pale in the center where they meet. Brush with more water to lighten if necessary.

Apply the vermilion paint.

6. While the fish is still wet, dip your brush into the raw sienna.

7. Make large spots across the body of the fish using the edge of the brush, and using the photo as a guide. Notice the spots get lighter as you move toward the tail.

Add brown spots.

8. Paint the gills and lower fins—pieces 2, 3, 4, 5, and 9—with vermilion.

9. Paint the tail and upper fin—pieces 6 and 7—with green-gold.

10. Paint the head to match the body by repeating steps 3 and 4.

11. Paint the upper and lower lips—pieces 10 and 11— with vermilion.

12. Dry all pieces with a hair dryer.

Assembly

1. Appliqué piece 12 (black) to piece 13 (yellow) for the eye and add to piece 9 (head).

2. Appliqué piece 11 (lower lip) to the head, matching raw edges and dotted outline.

3. Appliqué piece 10 (upper lip) to the head, matching raw edges and dotted outline.

4. Appliqué piece 9 to 8, then appliqué piece 8 to 1, and piece 1 to 6.

5. Appliqué lower fins—pieces 2, 3, 4, and 5—to the bottom of the fish.

6. Appliqué the upper fin—piece 7—to the top of the fish.

7. Press seams, trimming if necessary.

8. Make random dots on the upper fin, tail, and body with a black permanent marker.

9. Apply copper beech watercolor pencil around the eyes and mouth. Blend strokes with a damp cloth.

Brown Trout

Follow directions 1–10 for the Golden Trout, substituting yellow cotton fabric for the white. Continue following the directions below.

Painting

1. Lay all the pieces for the Brown Trout on the table, except for pieces 12 and 13 (eye parts), and spray with water until damp.

2. Mix one part green-gold paint to four parts water.

3. Paint the green-gold in one stroke across the body with a 1½" brush, starting at the top upper edge. Immediately dip your brush in water and blot on a paper towel. Brush across the bottom edge of freshly applied green-gold paint, blending toward the center of the body. Paint should blend from dark at the top to light toward the center. Rinse the brush.

4. Refer to the photo and paint all fins, tail, head, and gill pieces with the same green-gold paint.

5. Dry all pieces with a hair dryer.

Assembly

1. Assemble the same as the Golden Trout, following steps 1–7.

2. Using the black marker, make random dots on the body, head, gills, and upper fin.

3. Make slightly larger dots, mainly on the lower half of the body, with the yellow marker.

4. Using the red marker, make a smaller dot on top of all yellow dots.

5. Apply copper beech watercolor pencil around the eyes and mouth. Blend the strokes with a damp cloth.

Brook Trout

Follow instructions 1–10 for the Golden Trout except turn the templates over and use the wrong side so this fish swims in the opposite direction.

Painting

1. Lay pieces 1 (body), 7 (upper fin), 8 (gills), and 9 (head) on the table.

2. Apply color resist in a random dot pattern covering the upper three-quarters of the body. Cover the upper fin with dots, but apply dots sparingly to the upper part of the gills and head.

3. Be sure to let the resist dry thoroughly, which could take several hours.

4. Lay all pieces, except 12 and 13 (eye parts), on the table and spray with water until damp.

5. Three colors are used to paint the body of the fish. The lower part is painted with vermilion, the lower middle is painted with lemon yellow, and the upper part is painted with green gold.

6. Mix each color using the ratio of one part paint to four parts water.

7. Using a 1½" brush, paint the green-gold in one stroke across the body, starting at the top upper edge. Immediately dip your brush in water and blot on a paper towel. Using your brush, blend the paint from dark at the top to light toward the center. Rinse the brush.

8. Apply vermilion paint in the same way, starting from the bottom outside edge of the fish. Paint should blend from dark at the bottom to light toward the center. The two colors should be very pale in the center where they meet. Brush with more water to blend if necessary.

9. Paint one stroke of the lemon yellow across the body, just above the vermilion color. Blend the yellow into the green-gold above and the vermilion below.

10. Paint pieces 2, 3, 4, 5, 10, and 11 with the vermilion.

11. Paint pieces 6, 7, 8, and 9 with green-gold.

12. Dry all pieces thoroughly.

13. Soak all pieces with resist, following the manufacturer's instructions for the amount to use, in warm water, for about thirty minutes. Rinse until clean then dry.

Assembly

1. Assemble the same as the Golden Trout, following steps 1–7.

2. Fill in the white circles left by the resist with lemon yellow, using a small round brush.

3. Apply copper beech watercolor pencil around eyes and mouth. Blend the strokes with a damp cloth.

Finishing

1. Pin all fish to the background fabric and baste, referring to the photo and the assembly diagram.

2. Appliqué the fish, using the traditional needle-turn method or machine appliqué.

3. Transfer the lettering using a lightbox and disappearing pen.

4. Layer the top, batting, and backing together.

5. Hand quilt the lettering, and around each trout.

6. Square up the piece to finished size.

7. Apply binding.

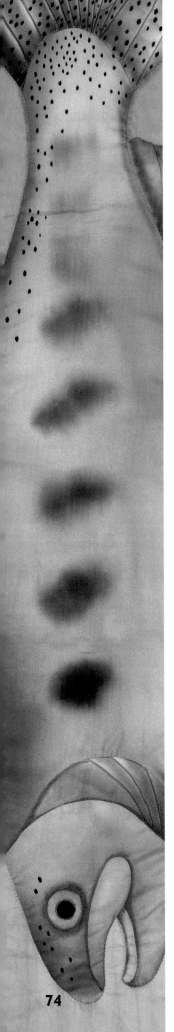

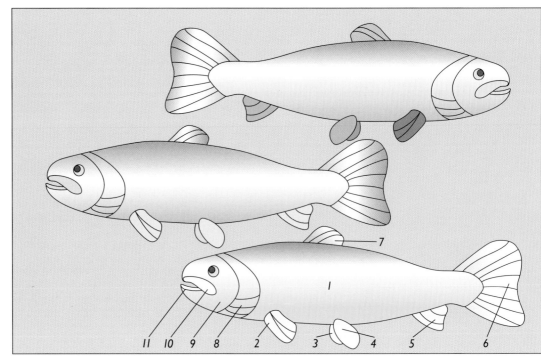

11 10 9 8   2   3   4   5   6

Assembly Diagram for Trout Study

Golden

Brown

Brook

Trout

Fin

7

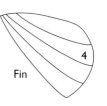

Fin

4

Fin

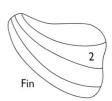

2

Fin

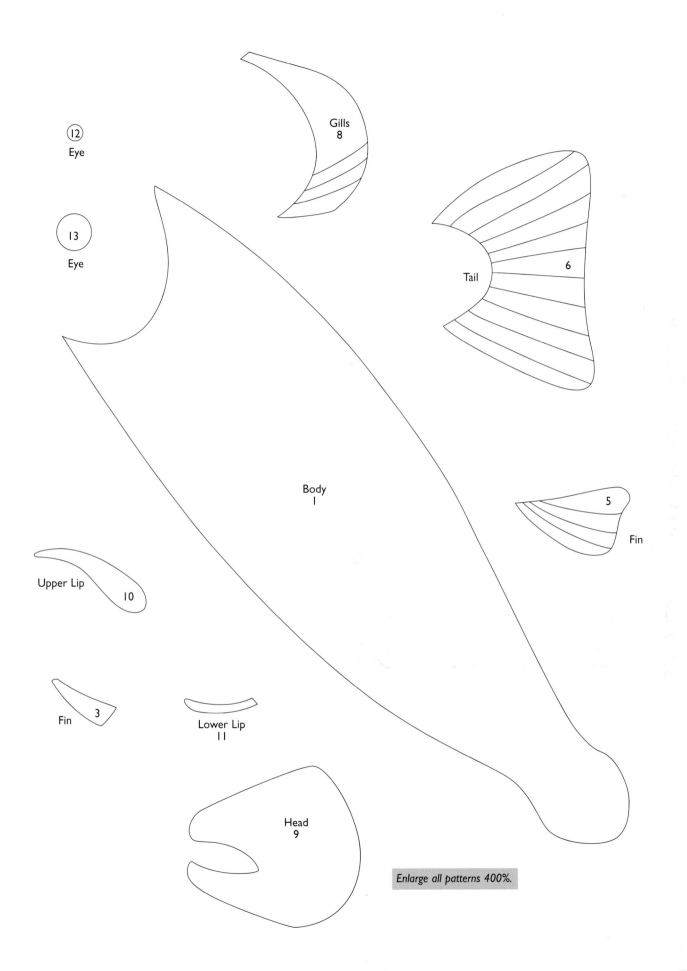

Gills
8

12
Eye

13
Eye

Tail

6

Body
1

5

Fin

Upper Lip

10

3

Fin

Lower Lip
11

Head
9

Enlarge all patterns 400%.

▲ *Catch of the Day*, 60" x 60", 1998
Techniques used: Tucks, Paint, Watercolor Pencil,
Water-soluble Crayon

▲ *Oceans*, 54" x 56", 1998
Techniques used: Tucks, Paint,

Author Biography

Velda E. Newman is a contemporary fiber artist from northern California. Her large-scale designs, portraying subjects from nature, have been exhibited extensively throughout the United States, Europe, and Japan. Velda uses textiles and thread the way other artists use paint and brush. Her primary source of inspiration is the natural world, and her exquisitely crafted quilts reflect the detail she finds there. Velda's quilt *Hydrangea* was awarded one of the Twentieth Century's Best American Quilts. Her work has appeared in many national and international publications and is included in both public and private collections. Velda lectures and teaches quilt-making in her own style of creating realism.

For more information, see *Velda Newman: A Painter's Approach to Quilt Design*, published by Fiber Studio Press (Martingale), 1996.

Index

◄ ***Bass in Your Dreams***,
79" x 86", 1999
Techniques used:
Tucks, Paint, Watercolor Pencil,
Water-soluble Crayon